The Book of Virtues
Book 1

Joanne Joefield

Trilogy Christian Publishers
A Wholly Owned Subsidary of Trinity Broadcasting Network
2442 Michelle Drive
Tustin, CA 92780

For information, address Trilogy Christian Publishing
Rights Department, 2442 Michelle Drive, Tustin, Ca 92780.
Trilogy Christian Publishing/ TBN and colophon are trademarks of Trinity Broadcasting Network.

For information about special discounts for bulk purchases, please contact Trilogy Christian Publishing.

Manufactured in the United States of America

10 9 8 7 6 5 4 3 2 1

Library of Congress Cataloging-in-Publication Data is available.

ISBN 979-8-88738-735-2 (Print Book)
ISBN 979-8-88738-736-9 (ebook)

I dedicate this book to my extended family, especially my mom Eulda,

who taught godly virtues to her offspring from sunup to sundown daily.

Torri Learns to Be Obedient

Torri was a five-year-old little girl who was loved by everyone. She was pretty and helpful and could say the funniest things that would make the saddest person laugh. She loved animals and plants, and continuously told people how much she cared for them.

Mommy and Daddy loved Torri very much and wanted the best for her. They gave Torri whatever she wanted, so after a while Torri began to grow very spoiled. Mom and Dad noticed her behavior, and occasionally they would discipline her if she did something wrong. Torri did not like this.

One day, she got disciplined for stomping her feet when Mommy scolded her. She was sent to her room for a "time-out" to think about her naughty behavior. Instead of obeying, she pouted and quietly slipped out of the house. She ran down the path, through the open gates, across the street, and into the park, way on the other side of her house.

There she sulked for a while, until she saw a beautiful little spotted pup. It was a Dalmatian puppy. It bounded up and down and chased the leaves on the ground. It ran this way and that, playing happily with anything and everything. Soon Torri was caught up with the delightful little animal, and they played happily together. They raced each other to the end of the fence and back, around the small pond, through the swings, behind various trees, and all the way down a narrow rocky path. Finally, they both lay panting, and Torri laughed happily as it rolled around on a soft tuft of grass.

After a while, in the distance there came a gentle bark, and the little pup's ears perked up. It listened and yelped back. Within a few moments the puppy's mother appeared, and both dogs ran off out of sight. Torri was now all alone, and for the first time she looked around and realized that she did not recognize her surroundings. It was very quiet, and there was no one else around. The sun had sunk very low in the sky, so Torri decided to head back home. But where was home? Which direction should she go? Around and around she turned, growing quite afraid.

Eventually, with tears in her eyes, she decided to walk in a particular direction that she thought would lead her home, but this only took her deeper into an unfamiliar area. Torri sat down and began to cry. She was lost, and she was very afraid. She had never been away from her home alone, or without an adult.

The evening grew darker, and Torri kept on walking, hoping to find or see something that was familiar to her. She saw nothing. She cried harder. What had she done? What had she gotten herself into? She just might never be found, and might never see Mommy or Daddy again! Oh, if only she had just obeyed and gone to her room! What an awful thing to happen! What was she to do?

But before she could cry any harder, she heard her name being called—softly in the distance at first, then louder as the voices came near. She answered as loudly as her little voice could and soon saw a group of people who included Mommy and Daddy.

As they got closer to her, she ran and threw her arms around her parents' necks, overjoyed that she was found. Daddy picked her up and kissed her puffy cheeks. Soon, they made their way home.

Torri apologized for her behavior and promised never to run away again. She promised to stop being so spoiled and disobedient.

Torri had learned her lesson; she knew that it was best to be obedient.

Biblical evidence of obedience:

In the book of Genesis, chapter 6, the Bible tells of God giving a godly man named Noah a command to build an ark (a huge boat/ship) to house animals and Noah's family. The other people at that time were wicked and did not obey how God wanted them to live.

God said that He was going to make it rain extremely heavily for a long time on the earth. This is called a flood—the earth was to be covered in water. Now it had not rained for a long time during Noah's time, and so Noah should not have been in a hurry to build a big boat. However, since God said it, Noah did it—he built the ark, and exactly how God wanted it built, too.

There is always a good reward for our obedience. When the flood came, Noah and his family and the animals chosen were shut safely inside the ark.

Just as our earthly parents require our obedience, even more so, God needs our obedience to Him at all times.

Bible verse on obedience:

Ephesians 6:1-3 (International Children's Bible)

Children, obey your parents the way the Lord wants. This is the right thing to do. The commandment says, "Honor your father and mother." This is the first commandment that has a promise with it. The promise is: "Then everything will be well with you, and you will have a long life on the earth."

Foot Learns How to be Patient

Foot was a very playful bear cub. He got his name because he would chase after any foot—or paw, or hoof, or any lower part of the body—as animals went by. Mama Bear had thought of calling him "Emerald" because of his beautiful but unusual green eyes, but the rest of the family thought that "Foot" was more appropriate.

One day, Foot asked Mama Bear to bake him a cake and cover it with honey. After all, honey was his favorite food. He loved honey so much that he sometimes wished to have it for breakfast, lunch, and dinner. However, his mother would explain that too much honey could make him sick. He would nod understandingly, but deep in his heart he longed for honey, honey, and more honey.

Mama Bear agreed to bake him his requested cake, but she asked him to be patient. Mama Bear was very busy these days, and so she promised to bake the cake one day soon. Foot was very happy and excitedly bounced off to chase after a foot or two.

Day after day, Foot reminded Mama Bear, and time and time again she would reply, "I haven't forgotten what I promised you. Just be patient a little while longer, Foot." And time and time again, he would say in a quiet voice, "All right, Mama."

Mama Bear's days became even busier, and Foot began to think that Mama had said she'd make the cake just to let him go off while she did her work. One day, after a week had passed, Foot decided to tell Mama exactly when he wanted his cake.

"Mama," Foot said, as she swept his bedroom floor. "I would like to have my cake on Monday, please."

"Very well, dear, that would be a good day to bake it," Mama answered, as she continued to sweep. Monday was two days away, and now Foot was more excited than before.

Monday morning Foot awoke early, because he could not help his excitement. He bounced out of bed and walked quickly to Mama and Papa Bear's bedroom door. After knocking, he hopped into bed with his parents and promptly awoke them.

"Mama," he cried, "it's Monday! You promised to bake me the honey-covered cake today, remember?"

"Yes, Foot," Mama Bear replied sleepily. "You'll have your cake today. Just be patient, little one."

After breakfast, Mama asked Foot to stay at home with Papa Bear while she visited Grandma. "Don't forget, you have to bake my cake," he reminded his mother, as he waved goodbye to her.

All morning he looked and looked for his mother to return, and by 11:00, he began to get quite impatient. Mama must have forgotten about her promise. She must have. Mama and Grandma Bear usually talked a lot when they got together. She really must have forgotten. At about noontime, Foot was convinced that Mama had forgotten all about him.

"Foot, come and have a bite to eat until Mama gets back. I know you must be hungry by now."

"No thank you, Papa," he sighed, wandering out to the backyard.

Foot kicked at pebbles and sighed heavily. His head hung low so that he saw only the ground before him. He was sad and wondered about Mama Bear.

"Hi there," shouted Al, a mischievous little bear-pal of Foot's. He was up a nearby tree. "What's the matter? Come on, it can't be all that bad."

"Yes, it is," Foot replied. "Mama promised to bake me a honey-covered cake today, but I think she has forgotten all about it, because she hasn't come back from Grandma's," Foot explained, broken-heartedly.

"Well," said Al. "You can come up and share my honey. Look what I've found!" Al promptly showed Foot the beehives of honey that he had found.

Foot's eyes grew big and without much hesitation, up the tree he climbed, as fast as his little paws could go. There he sat with his friend. They ate and laughed and talked together until they were filled.

"Thanks," groaned Foot, as he made his way down. "I'd better head on home. My tummy doesn't feel too good." And with that, Foot started home slowly.

Holding his tummy with one paw, he opened the front door with the other—and "SURPRISE!" came a chorus of voices. And surprised Foot was! It took him a while to respond, then he looked around and saw that the house was all decorated.

"Foot," cried Mama in the background. "It's your fifth birthday! Happy birthday, my little one!"

Foot was indeed surprised! Thinking very hard, he realized that it really was his birthday. As the crowd of his friends and family parted, he also saw the big cake, dripping with honey.

"Grandma and I baked this cake for you this morning at her house. I didn't want to do it here to give away the surprise party."

Papa took one look at Foot's face and knew that something was wrong. "What's the matter with your tummy?" he asked, seeing Foot's discomfort.

"I ate too much honey with Al, and I don't feel good."

"Oh no," cried Mama Bear. "I'm sorry that you are hurting, but I wish that you had just waited for me."

As Mama tucked Foot into bed, Foot wished with all his heart that he had been patient and waited for Mama. She usually kept the promises she made. He thought about all that Mama, Papa, and Grandma had done to celebrate his birthday. Now he had to listen to his party going on without him joining in the fun. At least, for a while, anyway…

Biblical evidence of patience:

There was once a man in the Bible, in Genesis 17, whom God promised to make a dad, since he did not have any children. His name was Abraham, and his wife's name was Sarah. They waited and waited and waited and waited, and they grew very old. Abraham was then one hundred years old, and his wife was ninety years old. They thought that it was impossible in their old age to have a baby. They made mistakes while they waited, just like the bear in our story above, but they eventually trusted God to keep His promise. It was a long wait, but wait they had to, because God was the only one who could answer their prayers correctly. God never goes back on His promises. Sarah soon realized that she was going to have a baby, and Abraham was very happy. In the end, they had their baby boy.

At times our loved ones, like our mom and dad, may promise us something and ask us to wait. We should do so. When we ask God for something also, we should trust Him, be patient, and wait for His answer. Showing patience while waiting on a promise can lead to a wonderful result.

Bible verses on patience:

Psalm 27:13-14 (NLT)

Yet I am confident I will see the Lord's goodness while I am here in the land of the living. Wait patiently for the Lord. Be brave and courageous. Yes, wait patiently for the Lord.

Psalm 40:1 (NCV)

I waited patiently for the Lord. He turned to me and heard my cry.

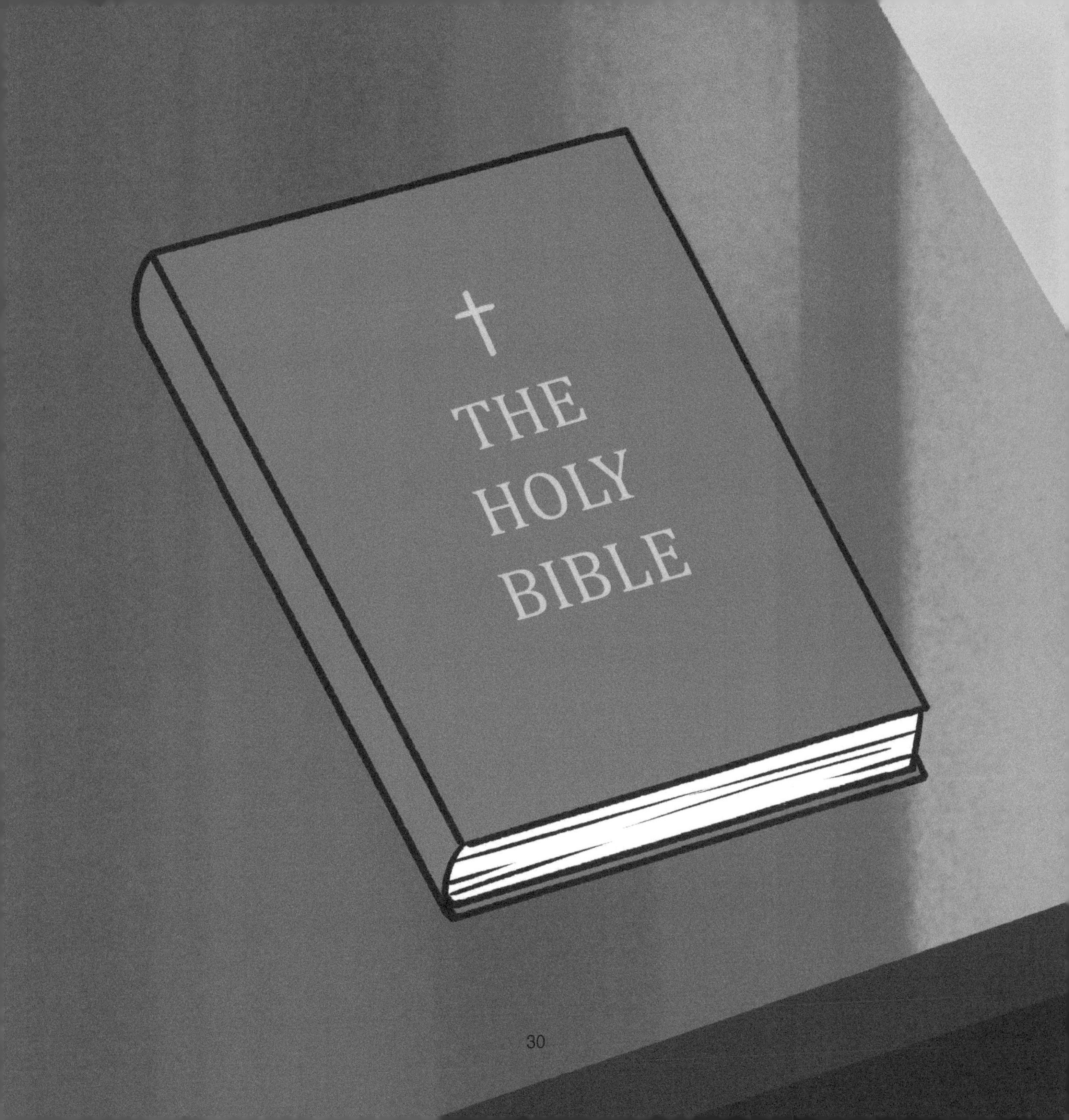
THE
HOLY
BIBLE

Milton Keynes UK
Ingram Content Group UK Ltd.
UKHW051850131023
430515UK00008B/36

9 798887 387352